Paint Recipes for Surfaces

Over 40 instant wall and floor transformations

Paint Recipes
for Surfaces

Over 40 instant wall and floor transformations

Stewart & Sally Walton

LORENZ BOOKS

First published in 2000 by Lorenz Books

© Anness Publishing Ltd 2000

Published in the USA by Lorenz Books
Anness Publishing Inc.
27 West 20th Street
New York, NY 10011
(800) 354-9657

ISBN 0 7548 0309 0

Publisher: Joanna Lorenz
Senior editor: Doreen Palamartschuk
Editor: Linda Doeser
Photographers: Graham Rae, Spike Powell, Mark Wood, Steve Tanner, Adrian Taylor,
Lucinda Symons, Rodney Forte, John Freeman
Stylists: Sacha Cohen, Catherine Tully, Diana Civil, Andrea Spencer, Fanny Ward,
Leean Mackenzie, Judy Williams
Illustrator: Madeleine David
Designer: Ian Sandom
Jacket designer: Clare Baggaley

Printed in Hong Kong/China

1 3 5 7 9 10 8 6 4 2

CONTENTS

INTRODUCTION 6

WALL PAINTING 8

DECORATING FLOORS 10

STENCILS AND STAMPS 12

INTRODUCTION

A COAT OF PAINT can transform a dark or shabby room, brightening it up and giving it a new lease of life without costing a fortune. But sometimes a plain painted wall lacks vibrancy and can be boring. The makeovers in this book change all that. Spending virtually the same amount of money and time as you would applying a simple coat of emulsion (latex), you can paint your lounge walls with a subtle two-toned effect, create the faded colours of a renaissance fresco in your bathroom and cover your kitchen with pink gingham squares. If your taste is for decorated walls, forget the misery of matching pattern repeats and handling messy wallpaper, and stencil a geometric border for a modern look or a wall full of colourful flags to brighten a child's room. Even easier, you can buy ready-made stamps in a huge range of designs or make your own. Simply roll paint on their surfaces and apply direct to the wall: as a single-design border, an alternating pattern or in conjunction with panels or other blocks of colour.

At a fraction of the cost of a new carpet, you can change the entire atmosphere of any room by painting the floor. Pastel stripes give a light, contemporary feel, and colourwashed parquet has a unique, understated elegance.

Cork flooring is warm, inexpensive and easily obtainable. Brighten it up by painting and stencilling.

Stencils and stamps work on floors as well, if not better, as they do to decorate walls.

Colour, whether on the walls or floor, is one of the most important elements in creating the mood of the room. You can choose your own combinations of shades for the techniques and projects in this book to evoke the atmosphere you want and be as bold or restrained as you like.

Vibrant blocks of contrasting colours on the wall, for example, have a lively, modern feel. The same project carried out in complementary pastel shades would create a tranquil and harmonious mood.

When you want a change, just turn to another project and get out the paint.

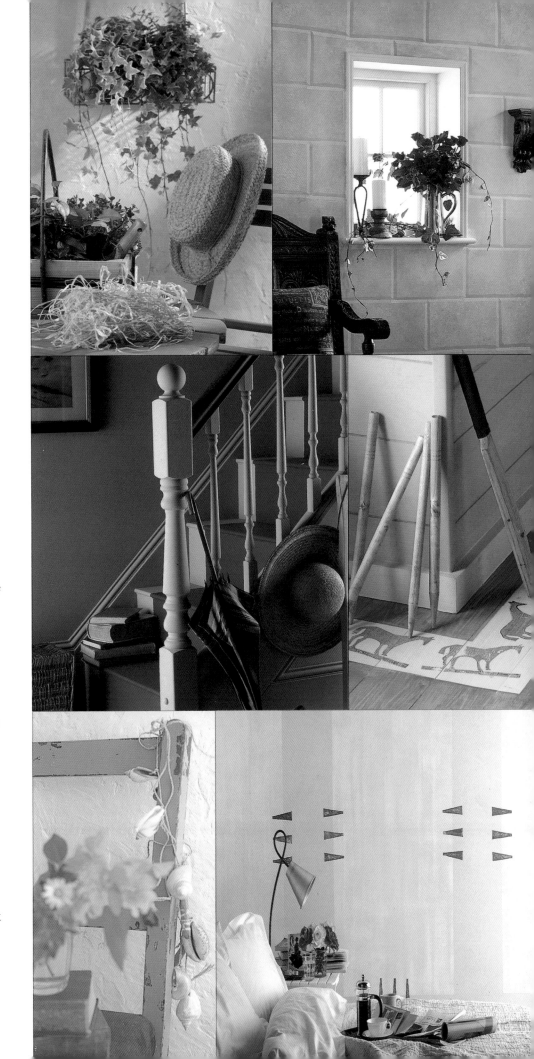

WALL PAINTING

Above: To achieve a strong Mediterranean effect, use a dark shade of blue colourwashed over a lighter shade. Colourwashing is ideal to cover a large expanse of wall.

A CLEVER USE OF COLOUR, painting techniques, borders and other decoration makes all the difference to any room. A coat of bright yellow paint can cheer up a room with little natural daylight, but using a wash of two shades of yellow is even sunnier and what light there is will bounce off the walls.

Light colours are said to make a small area look larger, but there can be other, more interesting solutions. Painting a darker colour above the level of the dado (chair) rail and a lighter colour below visually lowers the ceiling and widens the room. You do not need to

Right: This wonderful trompe l'oeil sky is glimpsed through window shapes and adds the illusion of space to the bathroom. Try it also on ceilings. The luminous quality is achieved by working down the surface several times, graduating the colour as you progress without adding more paint to the brush.

have a real rail, you could paint one or stencil or print a border at dado (chair) rail height to link the two areas together.

Although it is widely believed that walls must be in perfect condition for painting, this is not always the case. Colourwashing is just one technique that positively benefits from an uneven surface, creating a wonderful country feeling even in the city. Of course, some preparation is essential: walls must be clean and dust-free for the paint to adhere properly, crumbling plaster should be replaced and cracks filled. If the wall is in very bad condition, consider covering it up completely with tongue-and-groove and then painting that. Another interesting effect to try is painting the wall and then covering it with decorative perforated panels painted in a contrasting shade.

Above: This paint finish looks very dramatic in any room. Muted lighting catches the metallic diamond highlights.

Left: Frottage is the technique of texturing paint by pressing tissue paper over the wet surface. It is derived from the French, meaning "rubbing". Only the lightest touch is applied to the wet paint to ensure subtle tones of colour.

DECORATING FLOORS

Above: Transform old wooden floorboards by sanding them down and using a wood stain to create subtle variations in colour.

YOU CAN LET YOUR IMAGINATION run wild when painting floors. Multi-coloured striped floorboards and painted "tiles" are two very popular and easy techniques. An unpainted or plain-coloured floor looks wonderful with a border printed or stencilled around the edge, and this is a good way to add decoration without too much effort.

Floorboards can be painted directly or covered with sheets of hardboard, MDF (medium-density fiberboard) or cork tiles and then decorated. It is essential that any loose floorboards are nailed firmly in place and protruding nails are punched in. The floor must be clean and dust-free and, for the best effect, it is worth sanding it first. For a very delicate-looking finish or for preparing a badly stained floor, it may be worth hiring a commercial sander.

Right: Floor stripes can transform a room, adding a light playfulness on a minimal budget, and offer a lot of scope for versatile interior design.

Left: This checkerboard floor uses a contrasting terracotta and green. A combing technique has been used to vary the intensity of the colours and allow the grain to show through.

Although special floor paints are available, they are not essential. In fact, ordinary emulsion (latex) paint works very well and has the advantage of being easy to handle and quick drying.

Always work from the corner furthest from the door and paint your way out of the room. Let each coat of paint dry completely, at least overnight, before painting another coat, colour or decoration. When you have finished, apply a minimum of two coats of clear, hard-wearing polyurethane varnish, letting each one dry. If the floor gets a lot of use, such as in a hallway or kitchen, you may need to apply three or four coats of varnish.

Below: Make cork tiles in different colours to create a checkerboard effect.

STENCILS AND STAMPS

Above: This stencilled border visually integrates the two sections of wall and soften the edges between them.

THESE ARE THE EASIEST WAY to apply a unique decoration to walls, floors and other surfaces, such as ceilings. There are many ready-made designs available, and it is also easy to make your own.

Stencils can be made from acetate, which is transparent and is, therefore, easy to position accurately, or stencil card (stock). Cut them out with a scalpel or craft knife with a sharp blade to get a neat edge. Templates for the projects in this book are supplied, and these can be enlarged to the required size using a photocopier. Good sources for stencil designs are antique wallpapers; geometric shapes work well too and are easy to draw.

Right: This simple, yet stunning co-ordinated bedroom has been achieved by choosing a lavender-grey and white palette and using stamps to make matching accessories.

It is usually best to make a separate stencil for each colour. The paint should be almost dry; wipe off any excess with kitchen paper (paper towels) and, if in doubt, try the brush on a piece of scrap paper before beginning work. Stencil brushes have short bristles and are available in a wide range of sizes. Apply the paint by pouncing it through the stencil. Going over different areas more than once varies the depth of colour.

Stamps can be made from high-density foam. Attach your chosen template to the block of foam and cut around it with a craft knife to leave a raised design. You will not usually be able to do this in one go. Apply the paint to the stamp with a small roller and check that it is not too wet. Apply the stamp with an even pressure and lift it carefully afterwards to avoid smudging.

Above: A rubber stamp can be made to have several different characteristics, depending on the colours and inks that you choose.

Left: Use foam stamps to create this vibrant, colourful Mexican hallway. All sorts of homemade stamps can be made from high- and medium-density foam.

TWO-TONE ROLLERED WALL

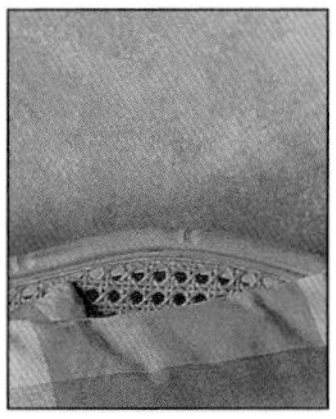

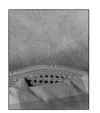

THIS INGENIOUS PAINT EFFECT produces a subtle mix and depth of colour. Two complementary shades of emulsion (latex) are placed next to each other in a paint tray and then rollered on the wall together over a cream-coloured base coat. Applying the roller in a variety of different directions blends the paint effectively. The painted surface resembles a cross between sponging and ragging, but this is a less laborious and time consuming technique. A light-handed touch is essential, as overworking the paint will destroy the subtlety.

YOU WILL NEED

paint roller
paint-mixing tray
emulsion (latex) paint:
cream, yellow and terracotta

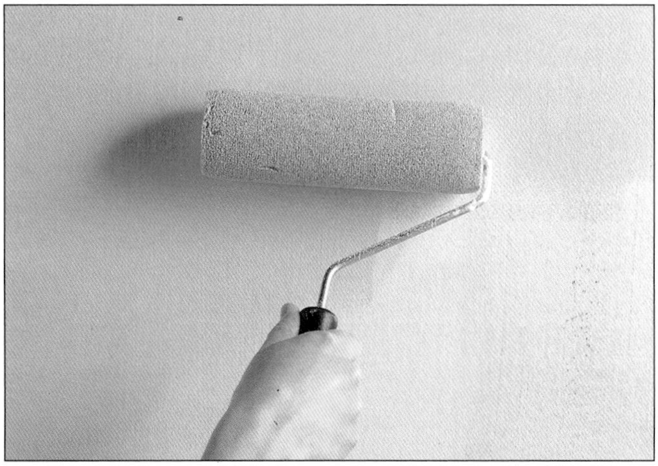

one *Paint the wall with a base coat of cream emulsion (latex) and leave to dry.*

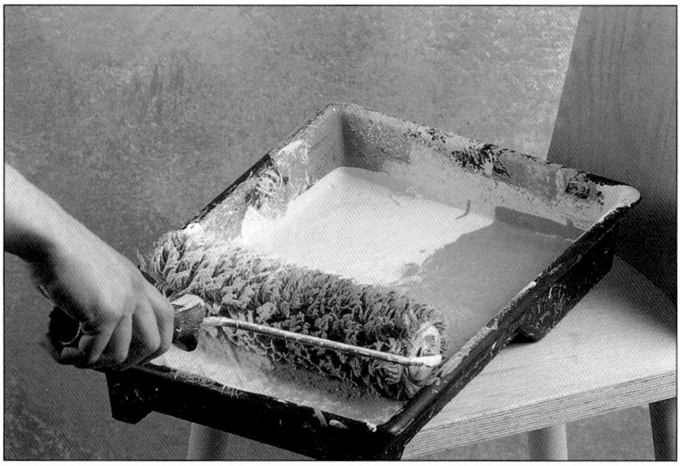

two *Pour the yellow and terracotta emulsion (latex) into the paint-mixing tray together, half on each side, so that the two colours are side by side without mixing.*

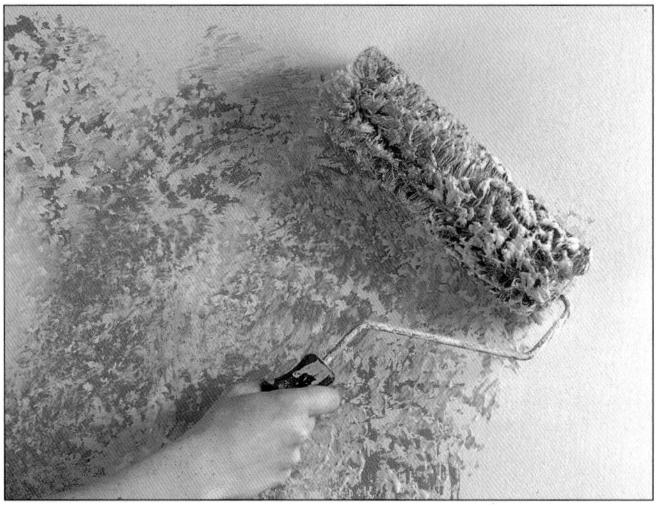

three *Paint the wall, applying the roller in a variety of different angles.*

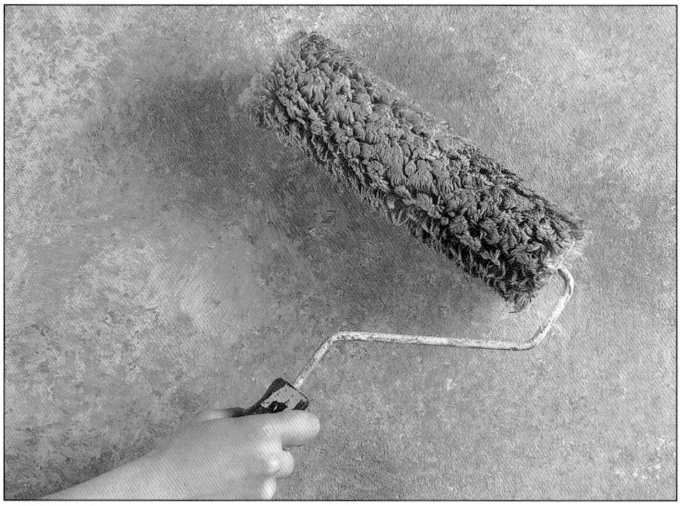

four *When the wall is completely covered, lightly roll over it a few times to blend the paint, but don't overwork.*

FROTTAGE HALLWAY

THE TECHNIQUE OF TEXTURING paint by pressing tissue paper over the wet surface is known as "frottage". Although derived from the French, meaning "rubbing", only the lightest touch is applied to the wet paint to ensure subtle tones of colour and a good bounce of light. Here, tone on tone in soft shades of green create the delicate effect shown on the walls above the dado (chair) rail. You will need to work on one manageable area at a time so that you can keep the edge wet. Better still, ask someone to assist you, one brushing and the other following with the tissue paper. The pattern of the textured wallpaper below the rail has been highlighted by stippling on a darker green glaze and then wiping it off with a cloth to reveal the raised areas.

YOU WILL NEED

silk finish emulsion (satin finish latex) paint:

light, medium and dark shades of soft green and white (buy a dark shade and mix it with white to make the light and medium shades)

large and medium household paintbrushes

matt emulsion (flat latex) paint:

medium shade of soft green

tissue paper

acrylic scumble

stippling brush

dry cotton cloth

one *Paint the upper part of the wall with two coats of light green silk (satin) finish paint, leaving each one to dry. Dilute the matt (flat) green paint with about 20 per cent water. Brush this on to a section of the wall.*

two *Immediately press a sheet of tissue paper over the entire wet surface, except for a narrow band adjacent to the next section to be painted.*

three *Carefully peel back the tissue paper to reveal the majority of the base colour.*

four *Brush two coats of medium green silk (satin) finish paint over the textured wallpaper, leaving each to dry. Mix dark green silk (satin) finish paint with acrylic scumble in a ratio of one part paint to six parts scumble. Brush this glaze on to a section of wallpaper.*

◄ **five** *Immediately lightly dab over the wet glaze with a stippling brush to eliminate brushmarks and even out the texture.*

six *Wipe a cotton cloth gently over the stippled glaze to remove it from the raised areas of the wallpaper. Paint the dado (chair) rail white, leave to dry and then brush the dark green glaze over the top.* ➤

Colourwashed walls

COLOURWASHING IS IDEAL for covering large, uneven surfaces quickly and easily. Not only can you experiment with colour – here colours reminiscent of the sea evoke an authentic ocean mood – but you can also try different textures. Applying the paint with a sponge, cloth, wallpaper brush, bunch of long feathers or a wide household brush creates a pleasingly different result each time. Pale colours work best on a white or off-white base, giving the feeling of a casually applied wash. To achieve a stronger effect, as here, use a dark shade for the base coat and an even darker tone over the top.

YOU WILL NEED

emulsion (latex) paint:
two shades of blue, one slightly darker than the other
household paintbrush
paint kettle (pot)
natural sponge
soft dry cloth (optional)

one *Apply two coats of the lighter blue to cover the surface, leaving each one to dry.*

two *Dilute the darker shade of paint with an equal quantity of water and apply it with a sponge in a circular motion.*

three *Rub over the edges with a soft cloth or sponge to avoid joins.*

four *Finally, dab paint in areas that are too light or show marks to give an even effect.*

FRESCO EFFECT

THIS TECHNIQUE CREATES THE FEEL of an Italian fresco painting with its "faded" colours and textured surface. This is achieved by using a dry brush to even out the brushstrokes after the glaze has been applied and then by rubbing with a dry cloth to produce the faded effect. It takes a little practice to manage the right action with the dry brush, which should be from the arm and not the wrist, and to apply the appropriate pressure. This wall treatment is the ideal background for a mural, so if you are feeling artistic, you could paint a scene on top.

YOU WILL NEED

emulsion (latex) paint:
pale pink and ultramarine

acrylic scumble

2 large household
paintbrushes

dry cloth

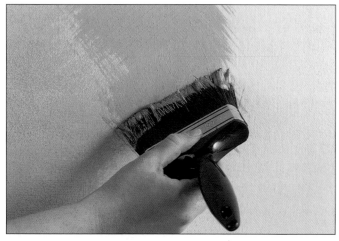

one *Mix a glaze with the pink paint and acrylic scumble in the ratio of one part paint to six parts scumble. Paint the glaze on to the top part of the wall with random brushstrokes.*

two *Using a dry brush, go over the top half of the wall to even out the brushstrokes.*

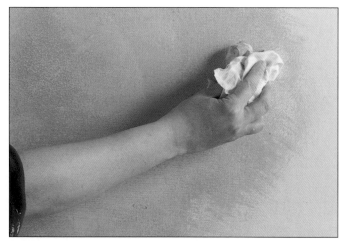

three *Rub a cloth into the glaze with circular motions to create a faded effect.*

four *Repeat the three steps on the bottom half of the wall using ultramarine paint and acrylic scumble. Softly blend the two colours together with a dry brush.*

BOLD BLOCKS OF COLOUR

FOR THE BOLDEST LOOK of all, paint vibrant blocks of colour all over the walls to create an effect like a painting by the Dutch cubist Piet Mondrian. Using a basic square grid, work across and up and down to create strong patterns and changes of colour. Although this example has been created in very brightly coloured paints, you could choose a more subdued or even subtle look, using complementary tones or much paler colours. Use this effect on all the walls in a room, if you're feeling brave, or confine it to one area, such as above a dado (chair) rail in a hall, for a less intense effect.

YOU WILL NEED

spirit (carpenter's) level

straight edge

pencil

scrap paper

emulsion (latex) paint in several colours

small and medium paintbrushes

masking tape

one *Draw a basic grid of squares directly on to the wall, using the spirit (carpenter's) level, straight edge and pencil.*

two *Decide on your colours. Putting small samples together on a sheet of paper may help you to decide which ones work together best.*

three *Mask off the areas for the first colour. The blocks can be squares or oblongs, and they can turn corners. Use as many or as few squares of the grid as you like.*

four *Paint the blocks. Remove the tape immediately and leave to dry. Repeat the process for each of the subsequent colours in your scheme.*

BRIGHT PLASTER WALL

WALLS CAN BE GIVEN new interest and depth with this technique, which has the additional advantage of hiding any minor blemishes or unevenness. The added dimension pleasantly alters an otherwise plain surface, and it is easily achieved with a little plaster filler scraped over the surface. For a much more subtle finish, the plaster filler can simply be added to the paint and brushed over the wall surface to give a very light texture. Here, a crisp white painted finish evokes whitewashed cottages by the sea, but the wall could just as well be washed over with any colour of your choosing. Experiment with turquoise and splashes of vermilion in furniture and soft furnishings, and revel in images of the sun-baked Mediterranean.

YOU WILL NEED
plaster filler

bucket

stirrer

piece of thick cardboard
or plywood

white emulsion (latex) paint

paint-mixing container
(optional)

household paintbrush

one *Following the manufacturer's instructions, mix the plaster filler in a bucket.*

two *Wipe it on to the wall with a piece of thick cardboard or plywood so that it forms an uneven surface. Leave to dry.*

three *When dry, apply a coat of emulsion (latex) paint, rubbing it in well with the paintbrush so that all the raised surfaces are thoroughly covered.*

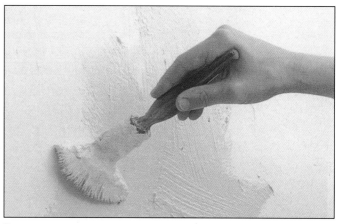

four *Alternatively, for a slightly smoother result, mix plaster filler and emulsion (latex) paint together and brush on.*

ROUGH PLASTER WASH

THIS SUNNY YELLOW WALL was given a rough-textured look by trowelling on a ready-mixed medium (joint compound) that is normally used for smoothing walls and ceilings that have unwanted texture. Colourwashing in two shades of yellow gives added depth and tone to create a light, carefree atmosphere. The absorbent wall surface picks up varying degrees of paint, and there will be some areas that are not coloured at all, but this is all part of the attractive rural effect. This technique would work equally well in a garden room that receives lots of natural sunlight and a small dark room in need of brightening up.

YOU WILL NEED

coating medium (joint compound)

plasterer's trowel or large scraper

large household paintbrush

emulsion (latex) paint: white and two different shades of bright yellow

household sponge

one *Apply the coating medium (joint compound) to the wall with a plasterer's trowel or large scraper, making the texture as rough as you like. Leave to dry overnight.*

two *Paint the wall with two coats of white, leaving each one to dry.*

three *Dilute one shade of yellow paint with about 75 per cent water. Dip a damp sponge into the paint and wipe it over the wall in large, sweeping movements. Leave to dry.*

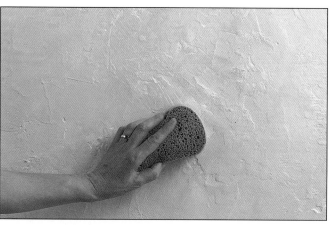

four *Dilute the second shade of yellow with about 75 per cent water and wipe it over the first colour in the same way.*

WALL BLACKBOARD

 THIS SIMPLE BLACKBOARD is lots of fun as well as being a highly practical wall treatment for a child's bedroom or playroom. Make sure the wall is flat before you start, and paint it with undercoat and two coats of emulsion (latex) first, if necessary. Bear the height of the child in mind when you are deciding on the size and position of the blackboard. Blackboard paint is available from most good paint suppliers.

YOU WILL NEED

tape measure

pencil

spirit (carpenter's) level

straight edge

masking tape

blackboard paint

paintbrushes

emulsion (latex) paint in
several colours

tracing paper (optional)

craft knife (optional)

self-healing cutting mat
(optional)

stencil brush

hooks

string

chunky (thick) chalks

one *Measure and draw the blackboard and the border on the wall, using the spirit (carpenter's) level and straight edge. Mask off the blackboard with tape and apply two coats of blackboard paint. Remove the masking tape immediately. Leave to dry.*

two *Mask off the border and paint with two coats of emulsion (latex). Remove the masking tape immediately.*

three *Mask off the diamond shape or draw and cut a stencil from tracing paper, using the craft knife and cutting mat. Tape it to the wall. Paint the diamonds with a stencil brush. Paint the hooks. Screw them into the wall and attach the chalks.*

$\mathscr{P}$AINTED BRICK HALLWAY

TURN YOUR HALLWAY into a welcoming area of serenity by decorating the walls with a dressed-stone effect reminiscent of an old country church. This easy technique relies on precision in drawing a grid to mark out the individual blocks before painting them in. Consistent edges of highlight and shadow define the blocks. To emphasize the church-like look, the cupboard is painted to give a dark oak effect. The rich depth of colour of solid oak is achieved by using burnt umber artists' oil colour paint.

YOU WILL NEED

sponge

emulsion (latex) paint in stone yellow, off-white and beige

spirit (carpenter's) level

pencil

paint kettle (pot)

wallpaper paste

1cm/½in flat end paintbrush

wooden cupboard

gloss or satin finish paint in beige

artists' oil colour paint in burnt umber

white spirit (turpentine)

fine graduated comb

heart grainer (graining roller)

cloth

large paintbrush

varnish

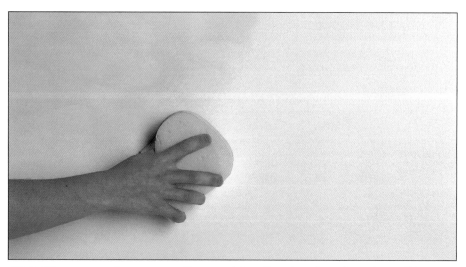

one *Dip a sponge into stone yellow emulsion (latex) and apply to the wall in a circular motion, creating an overall mottled effect.*

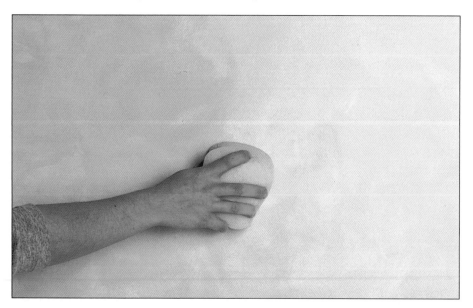

◄ **two** *Add a second coat of the stone yellow emulsion (latex) in patches and leave to dry. This will create a slight movement in the overall effect but will look almost solid.*

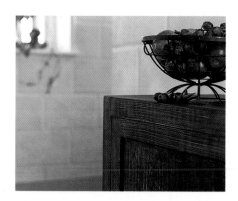

three *Using a spirit (carpenter's) level, draw a grid simulating the blocks to achieve a straight and accurate grid for the stone blocking effect.*

four *Mix off-white emulsion (latex) paint with 50 per cent wallpaper paste in a small paint kettle (pot). Using a 1cm (½in) flat end paintbrush, paint a stroke across the top and right hand of each block, beginning each line on a mitred corner. Leave to dry.*

five *Make sure the mitred corners are painted crisply.*

six *Mix beige emulsion (latex)paint with 50 per cent wallpaper paste in a small paint kettle (pot). Use the same flat end paintbrush to paint along the bottom and left of each block.*

➤

seven *To paint the cupboard, apply two coats of beige for the base coat in either gloss or satin finish and leave to dry thoroughly. Mix burnt umber artists' oil colour paint with white spirit (turpentine) in a paint kettle (pot) until it is the consistency of thick cream. Brush on and drag in a lengthways direction.*

eight *Using a graduated comb, pull down on the surface, not in totally straight lines, butting one up against the other.*

nine *Use a heart grainer (graining roller) to start making the details of the graining. Do this by pulling the tool down gently with a slight rocking motion, to create the hearts with random spacings. Butt one line straight over the other. Using a fine graduated comb, comb over all the previous combing.*

ten *Wrap a cloth around the comb and dab on to the surface to create the angled grain, pressing into the wet paint. Then, soften the overall effect using a large dry brush. Varnish when dry.*

NEO-CLASSICAL BATHROOM

AFTER A HARD DAY'S WORK, transport yourself to the relaxing atmosphere of the ancient Roman baths but with all the conveniences of modern living. This old cast-iron bath (bath tub) is painted with a marble effect on the outside that is easy to achieve, with enamel paint used as a base coat. Use a long-haired brush or feather to paint in veins, then soften them for a realistic subtle look. The wall panels are given a light *trompe l'oeil* sky effect, so that you have the impression of looking through columns or open window spaces to the exhilarating fresh air outside.

YOU WILL NEED

cast-iron bath (bath tub)

enamel (latex) paint in white

household paintbrush

artists' oil colour paint in Davy's grey (medium gray)

white spirit (turpentine)

paint kettle (pot)

long-haired artist's brush, swordliner (liner) or feather

large softener (blending) brush

varnish in gloss finish

silk finish emulsion (satin-finish latex) paint in white

emulsion (latex) paint in sky blue

sponge and pencil

wallpaper paste

one *To decorate the bath tub, apply two coats of white enamel paint to the outer surface of it.*

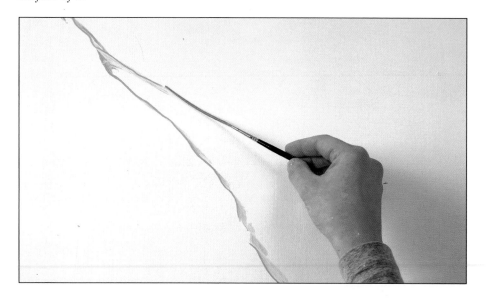

two *Mix a little Davy's grey (medium gray) artists' oil colour paint with white spirit (turpentine) in a small paint kettle (pot) until it is a thin creamy consistency. Use this mixture to paint in the fine veins of the marble with a long-haired artist's brush, swordliner (liner) or a feather.*

three *Soften the veins using a large soft brush to sweep over the lines.*

four *Add more veins, disregarding the positions of the first ones but working in the same general direction.*

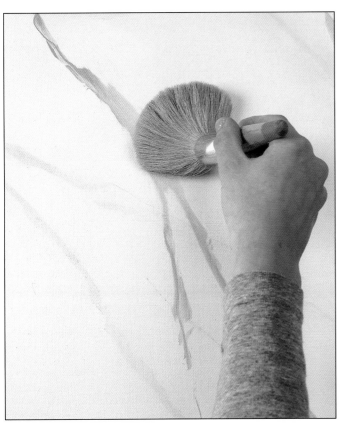

five *Soften these new veins with the large soft brush using only a little pressure this time, to give these ones a slightly stronger edge.*

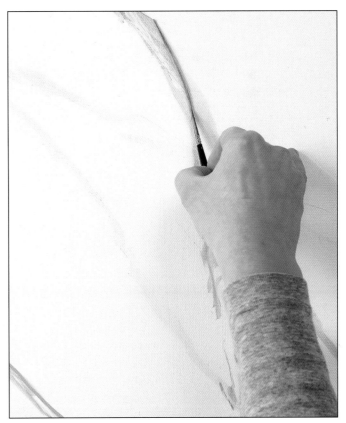

six *Using the same long-haired brush, add a defining line along the side of the second set of veins. Leave to dry. Varnish in a gloss finish.* ➤

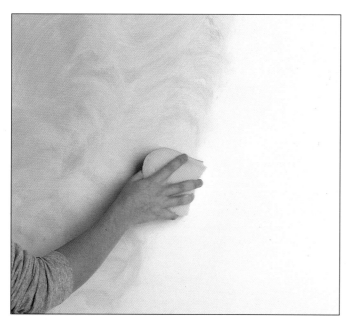

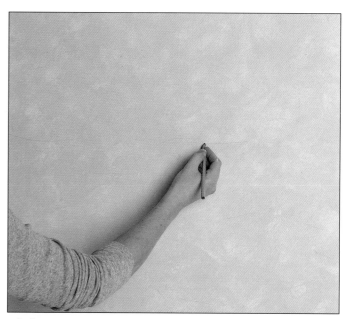

seven *To paint the walls, apply two coats of white silk emulsion (satin-finish latex) as a base coat, allowing to dry between coats. Dip a sponge into sky blue emulsion (latex) paint and rub over the whole surface in a circular motion, leaving a mottled effect. Apply a second coat of sky blue with a sponge in the same way. The second coat will leave the whole effect almost solid but slightly mottled in appearance.*

eight *Using a light pencil, carefully outline rough cloud shapes to give a guide for painting.*

nine *Dilute white silk emulsion (satin-finish latex) paint with 50 per cent wallpaper paste in a paint kettle (pot) and stipple this onto the surface, starting along the top edge of the pencil line. Continue to stipple downwards without applying any more paint to the brush, and this will gradate the colour. Build up the depth of the clouds in layers when each has dried, so go over the first layer along the top side and again stipple downwards. This will strengthen the effect.*

ten *Finally, add a more distinct, sharper edge to define the white of the cloud.*

LIMEWASHED WALL

FOR AN INSTANT LIMEWASHED EFFECT, apply white emulsion (latex) paint over a darker base with a dry brush, then remove some of the paint with a cloth soaked in methylated spirit (denatured alcohol). This is a good way to decorate uneven or damaged walls.

YOU WILL NEED

cream and white matt emulsion (flat latex) paint

2 large decorator's paintbrushes

old cloths

methylated spirit (denatured alcohol)

neutral wax

dry cloth

one *Paint the wall with a coat of cream emulsion (latex). Leave to dry.*

two *Dip the tip of the dry paintbrush into white emulsion (latex). Using random strokes, dry brush the paint on to the wall. Leave to dry.*

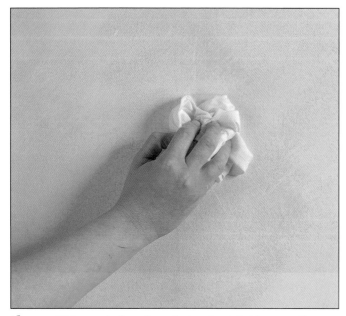

three *Using a cloth, rub methylated spirit (denatured alcohol) into the wall in some areas. Leave to dry.*

four *Using a dry, clean cloth, rub wax into the wall to seal the paint.*

PAINTED STAIRCASE

PAINTING A STAIRCASE in three strong colours makes into a central feature that will transform a room or hallway. For a co-ordinated look, repeat the colours on the walls. Gloss paint is normally used on stairs because it gives a thick, tough surface, but when it begins to chip off, it looks very scruffy. Here, ordinary emulsion (latex) has been used instead, painted over white primer. You can also paint directly on to bare wood when the paint wears; the wood will show through to give the distressed finish so typical of country style.

YOU WILL NEED

white acrylic primer

emulsion (latex) paint:

soft blue, mustard yellow
and brick red

medium and small
household paintbrushes

dust sheet (tarp)

masking tape

one *paint the wooden staircase with the acrylic primer. Paint the wall behind the staircase with blue emulsion (latex), continuing the colour a quarter of the way across the stair treads and risers. The edge will be painted over.*

two *paint the banisters and side panel with mustard yellow. Protect the rest of the staircase and floor with a dust sheet (tarp).*

three *Paint the outer skirting (baseboard) with blue, continuing the colour a quarter of the way across the stair treads and risers as in step one.*

four *Place strips of masking tape down the staircase, leaving an equal expanse of blue paint on either side. Paint the centre of the treads and risers with brick red. Paint the handrail brick red, leave to dry, then add a thin yellow line.*

DISTRESSED FLOORBOARDS

OLD WOODEN FLOORS ARE often appealing because of their subtle variations of colour. Wood stains can help to imitate that look in only a few hours. The look of driftwood, weathered teak or other hardwood decking, like that of beach houses, is the aim. Achieve the outdoor look using three different wood dyes and a wash of white emulsion (latex), heavily diluted with water. This technique gives a bleached effect to any wood stain.

YOU WILL NEED

nail punch

hammer

power sander and fine-grade sandpaper

wire brush

3 different wood stains of the same make

lint-free cloth or paintbrushes

rubber (latex) gloves

emulsion (latex) paint: white or cream

dry cloth

matt (flat) polyurethane floor varnish

one *It is important that floors have no sharp or protruding nails and so on, so knock in (pound) any you find with a nail punch and hammer before you begin. Remove old paint spills using a sander. Remember to change the sandpaper frequently, or you will damage the rubber seal of the sander.*

two *Brush the boards with a wire brush, along the direction of the grain, with the occasional cross stroke to give a distressed effect. Experiment with the stains, combining colours – a little should go a long way. Use scrap wood to test the effect before you commit yourself by staining the floor.*

three *With either a lint-free cloth or a paintbrush, apply the stain. This will stain anything porous, so wear rubber (latex) gloves and old clothes.*

four *Start by applying a generous quantity of stain, but rub most of the surplus off. Don't stop until you've finished the floor or there will be a definite line; keep the joins (seams) between areas random and avoid overlapping parallel bands of stain.*

five *It's better to do one thin coat all over and then go back to apply further coats. To give an uneven, weathered look you can work the stain into the knots or grooves with a brush.*

six *While the stain is still wet, brush on a wash of the diluted white or cream paint, about one part emulsion (latex) to four parts water.*

seven *Using a dry cloth, rub off any surplus or apply more until you have the effect you want.*

eight *Apply at least two coats of clear varnish, sanding very lightly between coats.*

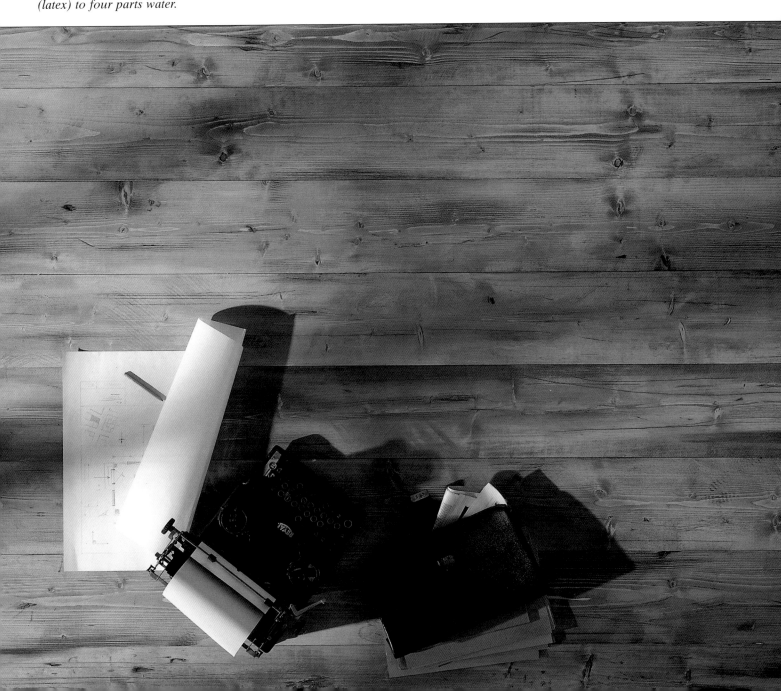

LIMED FLOORBOARDS

LIMING FLOORBOARDS creates a soft, weathered look that is reminiscent of a Scandinavian interior. This effect can also be achieved by simply bleaching the boards and scrubbing them vigorously every time you clean them. A quick, effective and less demanding way to whiten boards is to apply a coat of diluted emulsion (latex) paint or a mixture of pigment and linseed oil, although neither of these techniques is so long-lasting as liming.

YOU WILL NEED
wire brush
liming paste
fine steel wool
fine, clear paste wax
soft cloths

one *Stroke the floorboards with a wire brush, working gently in the direction of the grain.*

two *Apply the liming paste with some fine steel wool, making sure that you fill in the grain as you work.*

three *Working on a small area at a time, rub the liming paste into the boards in a circular motion. Leave to dry thoroughly.*

four *Remove the excess by rubbing in some clear paste wax with a soft cloth. Buff the surface with a soft cloth to give a dull sheen.*

PASTEL STRIPES

FLOOR STRIPES CAN TRANSFORM a room, adding a light playfulness on a minimal budget, and offer a lot of scope for versatile interior design. For maximum effect, keep your furnishings light and fun, adding bright patches of unexpected colour with small objects, such as vases, chairs and ornaments. The alternating colours also allow you to bring in different cushions and curtains for the various seasons. For a nursery and child's room, substitute bold reds, blues, orange, yellow and greens for these pastel colours.

YOU WILL NEED

nail punch

hammer

power sander and fine-grade sandpaper

masking tape

pencil (optional)

eggshell matt (oil-based satin-finish) paint:

lemon, pastel blue, pink and green

household paintbrushes

matt (flat) varnish

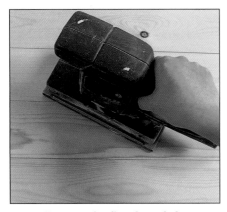

one *Prepare the floorboards by knocking in (pounding) any protruding nails with a nail punch. Remove old paint spills using a sander and sand the boards thoroughly. Test your colour combination on a separate board.*

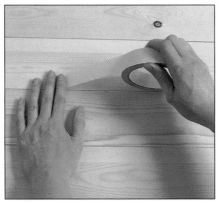

two *Mask along the edges of every alternate board. You may find it helpful to indicate your colour choice on each board in pencil, so you don't lose track of the repeat order.*

three *Starting with the lightest colour, paint all the boards in between the ones edged with the masking tape. Leave the paint to dry, then remove the tape. Mask along the edges of the painted boards. Paint all the boards in this way.*

four *Finally, when the stripes are completely dry, apply two or three coats of varnish to seal.*

CHECKERBOARD FLOOR

PAINTING A PATTERNED FLOOR may seem quite a daunting task, but stunning results, such as this combed design, will bring you endless compliments. The materials are inexpensive compared to the price of carpet, and while time and care are required, the painting is not difficult. If the room is large, use a straight edge to check the grid lines. A cardboard square cut to the size of the actual finished squares can also help you to align the design. Start painting in the corner farthest from the door and paint your way out of the room.

YOU WILL NEED

several pieces of thick mounting (mat) board

craft knife

white emulsion (latex) paint

large and medium household paintbrushes

tape measure

2.5cm (1in)) wide masking tape

long straight edge (optional)

38cm (15in) cardboard square (optional)

artist's acrylic paint: terracotta and green

clear matt (flat) polyurethane varnish and brush

one *Cut V-shaped teeth along one edge of each piece of mounting (mat) board to combs. The combs will soften with use.*

two *Paint the floor with white emulsion (latex). When dry, place masking tape all around the edge of the room.*

three *Using a tape measure, mark 40cm (16in) squares on the masking tape. Start in the most visible corner, measuring half a square 20cm (8in) in each direction.*

four *Lay down a grid of tape lines. Use a straight edge and/or the cardboard square, if necessary, to keep the squares even.*

five *Experiment on a piece of cardboard to find the amount of paint most suitable for combing. Apply the paint to the floor, alternating the choice of colours.*

six *Press a comb down into the paint, wiggling it from side to side to vary the pattern. Wipe off the paint when the comb begins to clog, and replace with a new comb when necessary. Leave to dry completely, then remove the tape. Apply two coats of varnish, leaving each one to dry.*

POP-ART FLOOR

MUCH INSPIRATION for interior decoration is to be gleaned from the pop artists of the 1960s, with their whimsical approach to art. These naïve shapes painted on a large surface make use of the pop-art conventions of sheer boldness and simplicity, with multiple repetitions of strong images rather than intricate busyness. Dramatically discordant colours – orange and shocking pink in this case – are the most appropriate. This idea works best on a concrete floor.

YOU WILL NEED

matt emulsion (flat latex) paint: white, blue, red, shocking pink and orange

paint roller

tape measure

pencil

masking tape

PVA (white) glue or acrylic varnish

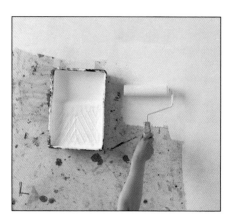

one *Give the floor two coats of white paint, to ensure that the colours of the design ring bright and true.*

two *Measure and draw out your design. Mask off the border, which needs to be crisply painted. Do the same along the outside of the star.*

three *Paint the star, then fill in the area inside the border; masking may not be necessary, as a little white space between the star and border and back-ground makes it look as though silk-screening has been used – a technique common in pop art. Seal the floor with diluted PVA glue or acrylic varnish.*

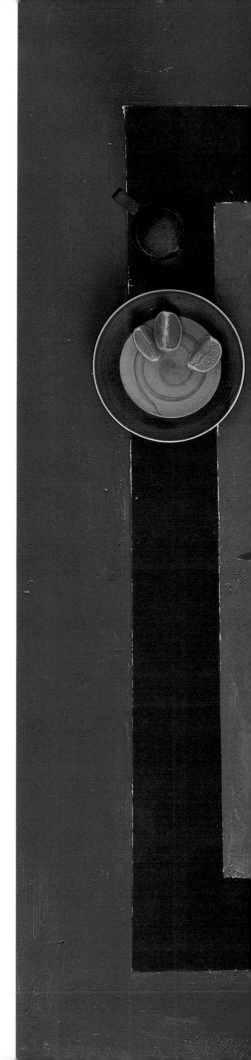

WOOD-GRAIN FLOORING

CHECKERBOARD FLOORS ARE a popular theme for flooring but are rarely seen in natural wood. If you are starting from a concrete or wooden floor, have the new floor covering cut into squares the size you want. If your floor is already covered in sheets of plywood, fibreboard or hardboard, mark a checkerboard pattern, ignoring the natural seams. Woodgraining does not have to be done painstakingly carefully. Obtain a sample of the wood effect you want; we used oak, grained to resemble wood treated in different ways, half "polished" and half "rough-sawn and sandblasted". You can use two different wood effects if you wish.

YOU WILL NEED

pencil

tape measure

long ruler or straight edge

masking tape

oil-based eggshell (satin-finish) paint: two shades of cream

paintbrushes

wood sample

artist's oil paint to match wood sample

oil-based scumble or glaze

paint thinner

dry-graining brush

graining comb

satin varnish

soft cloth

non-slip polish

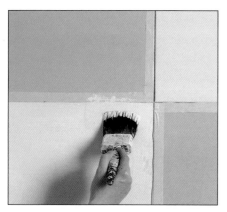

one *Make sure the surface is smooth and mark into checkerboard squares. Edge alternate squares with strips of masking tape and paint them, using two different cream eggshell paints.*

two *Mix the oil colours into the glaze, to match the wood sample. Thin if necessary. For the "lighter" squares, brush on the glaze in the direction you want the grain to run.*

three *Add random strokes, allow to dry for a few minutes and then drag a dry-graining brush over the glaze to give the graining effect.*

four *To introduce the chevrons of the wood grain, use a darker oil paint and draw them in with a fine artist's brush. Soften with a broad brush, adding thinner if the paint has dried.*

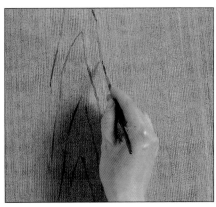

five *Soften the chevrons with a broad brush, adding some thinner if the paint has dried.*

six *For "darker" squares, repeat step 2 and then 3, using a graining comb rather than a dry-graining brush so the grain looks wider. Paint on darker chevrons as before, following the grain of the glaze.*

seven *Soften the effect, using the graining comb, then the brush. Apply two coats of satin varnish and allow to dry. Burnish with non-slip polish.*

COLOURWASHED PARQUET

HERRINGBONE PATTERNS ON FLOORS give instant classical elegance, suggestive of the wonderful dark oak parquet floors found in large old houses. However, a fresher look is often wanted, yet with all the interest of the old floors; the introduction of a pale, soft colour lifts gloomy dark wood into the realms of light Atlantic beach houses or modern Swedish homes. To keep the interest of the grain of the wood running in different directions, paint each individual piece separately.

YOU WILL NEED

marine-plywood, cut into manageable lengths

mitre saw

tape measure

sandpaper

matt (flat) emulsion (latex) paint: cream, blue and white

paintbrushes

matt (flat) water-based glaze

lint-free cloth

string

pencil

ridged adhesive paper

PVA (white) glue floor adhesive

matt (flat) varnish

one *Make sure the floor is clean, dry and level. Mitre the edges of the marine-plywood strips, using a mitre saw. Remember that you must have left- and right-hand mitres in equal numbers. Measure your required length for the herringbone pattern and cut as many as you need for the floor.*

two *Smooth any rough edges with sandpaper. Undercoat all the boards with cream matt (flat) emulsion (latex) and allow them to dry completely.*

three *Mix up at least four variations of blue with a very slight tonal difference between them. Add a little matt water-based glaze to each, to delay the drying time. Thin one of the colours with water to make it even more translucent. Paint equal numbers of the boards in each colour.*

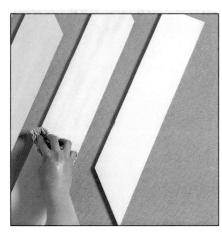

four *With the lint-free cloth, wipe off most of the paint randomly while it is still wet, so that the undercoat shows through. Wipe in the direction of the grain of the wood.*

five *Sand some areas of some boards when the paint is dry; this will give a contrast when the floor is down. Mark guidelines on the floor with stretched string and a pencil. Lay the floor using ridged adhesive spreader and floor adhesive, and apply the parquet blocks. Make sure they all lie flush. Finally, seal the whole floor with at least two coats of matt (flat) varnish.*

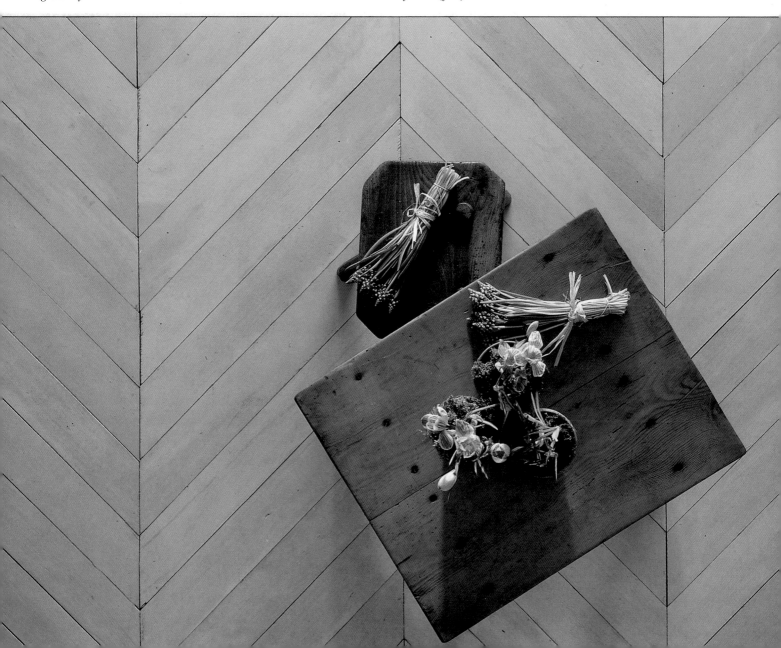

GROOVED FLOOR

TONGUE-AND-GROOVE BOARDS look wonderful with a gleaming shine. Gloss paint or floor paint is durable and easily renewed if it's ever damaged. Use this floor in a room with a large window and enjoy the dramatic effect of the sun streaming across it. Gloss paint shows up detail, so it was a natural choice for these brand-new tongue-and-groove boards, but if you like the effect of the dramatic colour but have a an old, beaten-up floor, a matt (flat) varnish would be more forgiving. To lay a new floor of this type, a perfectly smooth and level subfloor is vital.

YOU WILL NEED

tongue-and-groove boards
hammer
drill, with pilot drill bit
flooring pins and hammer
nail punch
power sander and sandpaper
undercoat paint
paintbrushes
high-gloss floor paint

one *Slot the tongue-and-groove boards together and, using an offcut (a scrap) to protect the exposed tongue, tap the next board into place until it fits tightly. If the boards are warped, pin one end first and work along the board; in this way you will be able to straighten out the warp.*

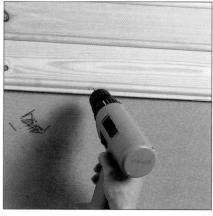

two *To prevent the tongues from splitting, pre-drill pilot holes. Tap pins in gently, using a pin hammer, at a slight angle back towards the boards.*

three *Punch the pins in with a nail punch so the next board can butt up.*

four *When the floor is laid, and before finishing it, sand it, first with a coarse-grade sandpaper and then with medium-grade and finally with fine-grade. Always sand in line with the wood grain. With long, even strokes, in line with the boards, undercoat the floor. Leave to dry. Lightly sand again and paint with gloss paint.*

TEXTURED GOLD FLOOR

SOUVENIRS FROM FAR AWAY places sometimes require a dramatic backdrop to set them off. Gold and copper are suitably flamboyant, but texture is also needed. Builders' scrim, used to reinforce plaster, fits the bill. It gives a surface that traps different amounts of gold and copper, creating the effect of beaten metal. As with all exotic finishes, the delight is more in the instant transformation than in practicality.

YOU WILL NEED

tape measure

pencil

paper

ruler

power sander, with fine-grade sandpaper

builders' scrim

scissors

PVA (white) glue

oil-based gold paint

wide paintbrush

copper powder paint

heavy-duty floor varnish

one *Measure the floor. Take into account the width of the scrim, plan your design on paper first to make sure that your pattern doesn't leave awkward half lines at the edges. You may need to lay marine-plywood or hardboard to ensure a smooth, flat surface. Lightly sand the floor to make sure it's perfectly flat.*

two *Cut the lengths of scrim, starting with the longest, and lay it to your pattern. Conceal joins (seams) where two lengths cross underneath, over-lapping the ends by at least 15cm (6in).*

three *Stick the scrim down with PVA (white) glue. Brush out any glue that soaks through to the top to hold the scrim firmly. Don't worry if you spread glue outside the area of the scrim. Pencil in a few guidelines and put a weight on the other end of the scrim to keep it straight. Dilute the glue with water and coat the whole floor. This seals the floor and forms a key for the paint.*

four *Paint on the gold paint with the wide brush, covering the whole floor. If using an oil-based paint, ensure that you work in a well-ventilated room.*

five *Allow the floor to dry. Dust the copper powder paint over the scrim, allowing it to be trapped by the mesh surface. Apply at least two coats of heavy-duty floor varnish to seal.*

FAUX-SOAPSTONE FLOOR

BLACK CORK TILES covering the whole floor in this room were too severe, but when the middle section of the room was treated to this soapstone effect, they became an important part of the overall grand gesture. The cork tiles in the centre were replaced with a large piece of MDF (medium-density fiberboard), to which a maze pattern was applied. This could have been painted on to plywood or MDF as a two-dimensional effect, but here the surface has been enhanced by routing the maze pattern (take it to a local joiner; routing really isn't for the inexperienced) and then painted to create a soapstone effect. You could also imitate slate, by using a wave formation and the black leading that was used in the nineteenth century for cleaning cast-iron fireplaces and grates. Sand or prepare your floor before beginning.

YOU WILL NEED

paper

pencil

MDF (medium-density fiberboard) sheet

plastic wood or wood filler, if necessary

fine-grade sandpaper

matt emulsion (latex) paint: white, dark grey and mid (medium)-grey

paintbrushes

wax candle

scraper

softening brush

matt (flat) varnish

one *On a new floor, plan your design on paper, using this picture as a guide. Draw it on to the sheet of MDF (medium-density fiberboard). Take it to a joiner to be routed and ask him to fix it in place on your floor. On an existing floor, draw the maze on the floor directly and ask a joiner to do the routing in situ.*

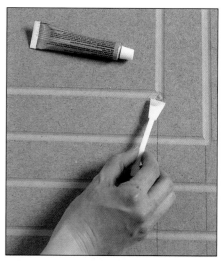

two *Fill any damage with plastic wood or wood filler, following the manufacturer's instructions. Don't try to achieve a perfectly flush surface at this stage. Leave to dry.*

three *When dry, gently sand until you have a level surface.*

four *Paint the whole surface white and allow it to dry.*

five *Paint over the whole surface of the floor in dark grey.*

six *Using a candle, apply a generous coating of wax with circular movements to the surface of the floor.*

seven *Take off most of the candle wax, using a scraper.*

eight *Follow this with a coat of mid (medium)-grey paint.*

➤

nine *Apply another coat of wax. Take off the wax with the scraper.*

ten *Apply white paint with a dry softening brush to soften the whole effect. Seal with matt varnish. If you are surrounding the board with cork tiles, lay them at the end and butt them up to the edges neatly.*

DIAMOND-STENCILLED WALL

HERE A STUNNING COLOUR SCHEME is created by dragging a deep green glaze over a lime green base. The surface is then stencilled with shiny aluminium leaf diamonds, which stand out against the strong background. This paint finish would look very dramatic in a dining room, with muted lighting used just to catch the metallic diamond highlights.

YOU WILL NEED

2 large decorator's paintbrushes

lime green emulsion (latex) paint

monestial green and emerald green artist's acrylic paint

acrylic scumble

pencil

stencil card (stock)

craft knife

cutting mat or thick card (cardboard)

2 artist's paintbrushes

acrylic size

aluminium leaf

make-up brush

clear shellac

one *Using a large decorator's brush, paint the wall with lime green emulsion (latex). Leave to dry. Mix a glaze from 1 part monestial green acrylic paint, 1 part emerald green acrylic paint and 6 parts acrylic scumble. Paint the glaze on to the wall with random brushstrokes.*

two *Working very quickly with a dry brush, go over the wall surface with long, downward strokes. Overlap the strokes and don't stop mid-stroke. Leave to dry.*

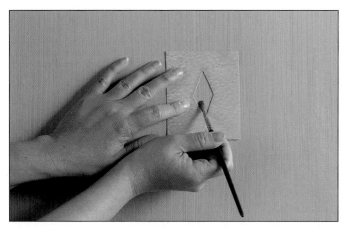

three *Draw a small diamond shape in pencil on to stencil card (stock). Cut out, using a craft knife and cutting mat or thick card (cardboard). Using an artist's paintbrush, apply a thin, even coat of acrylic size through the stencil card (stock) on to the wall. Repeat as many times as desired to make a decorative pattern.*

four *After about 20 minutes, touch the size lightly with a finger to check that it has become tacky. Press a piece of aluminium leaf gently on to the size.*

◄ **five** *Working carefully, peel off the aluminium leaf, then brush off the excess with the make-up brush.*

six *Using an artist's paintbrush, apply shellac over the diamond motifs. Leave to dry.* ➤

STAR STENCIL

THIS MISTY BLUE COLOUR SCHEME is ideal for a bathroom or washroom, and the lower part of the wall is varnished to provide a practical wipe-clean surface. The tinted varnish deepens the colour and gives it a sheen that contrasts beautifully with the chalky-blue distemper above. The stencil is based on a traditional quilting motif and is very simple to create.

YOU WILL NEED

paper and pencil

straight edge

scissors

spray mount adhesive

stencil card (stock)

sharp craft knife and cutting mat

soft blue distemper or chalk-based paint

household paintbrushes

spirit (carpenter's) level

straight edge

clear satin water-based varnish

varnish brush

Prussian blue artist's acrylic paint

star template (page 94)

one *Draw the star shape on paper using the template. Spray the back lightly with adhesive, then stick it on to the stencil card (stock).*

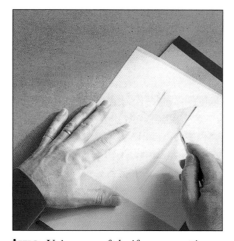

two *Using a craft knife on a cutting mat, cut out the star. Cut inwards from the points towards the centre so that the points stay crisp.*

three *Peel off the paper template to reveal the stencil.*

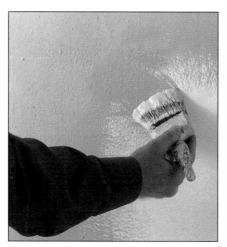

four *Dilute the blue paint, if necessary, according to the manufacturer's instructions. Brush it on to the wall with sweeping, random strokes to give a colourwashed effect.*

five *Using a spirit (carpenter's) level, and a straight edge ruler, draw a pencil line across the wall at the height you want to finish the varnished surface.*

◄ **six** *Tint the varnish with a squeeze of Prussian blue acrylic paint. Using a separate brush, apply this on the lower part of the wall up to the marked line.*

seven *Spray the back of the stencil lightly with adhesive and position at one end of the wall, about 5cm (2in) above the marked line. Stencil with the tinted varnish, using a broad sweep of the brush. Repeat along the wall, spacing the stars evenly.* ➤

FLAG STENCILS

HERE'S A STRONG DESIGN to add lively colour and an element of fun to a child's room, while avoiding the conventional and rather predictable motifs and colours available in ready-made children's wallpapers. The easiest way to make a unique stencil is to photocopy a simple motif on to acetate: here, two complementary flag motifs are combined. Use the stencils as a border at picture- or dado (chair) rail height, randomly around the room or in straight lines to make a feature of, for example, a chimney breast on one wall or an alcove behind a desk or bookshelves.

YOU WILL NEED
acetate sheet

craft knife

self-healing cutting mat

sticky tape

stencil brush or small paintbrush

emulsion (latex) paint: black and several bright colours

one *Photocopy the designs from the back of the book in various sizes to try them out. When you are happy with the size, photocopy them directly on to the acetate.*

two *Cut out the stencils carefully, using a craft knife and cutting mat. Tape the stencil to the wall.*

three *Stencil a bold outline in black.*

four *Use a stencil brush to apply colour inside the outline, or paint it free-hand for a looser, more appropriate effect for a child's room.*

STENCILLED BORDER

THIS DESIGN IS BASED on a border from the eighteenth century, when stencilling was an extremely popular means of decorating interiors. This is perfectly suited for use above a dado (chair) rail, but there is no reason why you should not use it at picture rail or skirting board (baseboard) height, or even as a frame around a window. Or you may not have a dado (chair) rail, but still like the effect of a wall divided in this way. In that case, it is simply a matter of marking the division with paint or varnish, as shown here. The stencilled border will then visually integrate the two sections of wall and soften the edges between them.

YOU WILL NEED

Template

tracing paper

acetate or stencil card (stock)

pencil

spray adhesive

scalpel or craft knife

emulsion (latex) paint (colours optional)

varnish in shade "Antique Pine" (optional)

stencil paint

stencil brush

kitchen paper (paper towels)

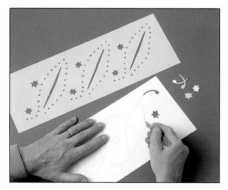

one *Trace and enlarge the design from the back of the book. Stick it on to acetate with spray adhesive and cut out with a scalpel or craft knife. Peel off the remaining tracing paper.*

two *Paint the whole wall in your chosen colour. Paint the lower half of the wall with a coat of Antique Pine varnish, if using. Use random brush strokes for a rough finish.*

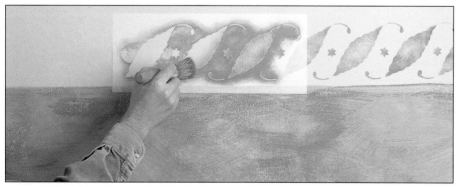

three *Lightly spray the back of the stencil with adhesive and leave for 5 minutes. Position the stencil at a corner and paint the first colour. Use the paint very sparingly, wiping the brush almost dry on kitchen paper (paper towels) before using it on the walls. Lift the stencil and wipe away any excess paint from the pattern edges before positioning it alongside the stencilling. Continue along the walls at dado (chair) rail height until the first colour is complete.*

four *As stencil paint is fast-drying, you can immediately begin to add the next colour, starting at the same point as the first. Work your way around the border, remembering to wipe the stencil clean as you go.*

PANELS AND STAMP MOTIF

BRING LARGE AREAS OF DECORATION to a wall with these easy panels. Painting or dragging (strié) panels over a base coat quickly gives interest to large expanses of wall. It's a good idea to connect the panel and wall area outside visually with a simple motif. This could be a strong modern shape, wavy lines or even flowers. The colour of the walls and the style of the motif give scope for a wide range of different looks from the same basic treatment and, of course, you can vary the size of the panel to fit the shape and dimensions of the room.

YOU WILL NEED

emulsion (latex) paint in cream, white and black

paint roller

paint-mixing tray

spirit (carpenter's) level

straight edge

pencil

masking tape

dragging (strié) brush

scrap paper

scissors

high-density foam

glue

craft knife

tape measure

old plate

small roller

one *Coat the wall with a base of cream emulsion (latex) paint. Using the spirit (carpenter's) level and straight edge, draw the panels on the wall when dry.*

two *Mask off the outer edge of the panels with masking tape. Drag (strié) white emulsion (latex) paint over the base coat.*

three *Design the motif on paper. Stick the motif to the foam. With the craft knife, cut out the unwanted areas of the design to leave a raised stamp.*

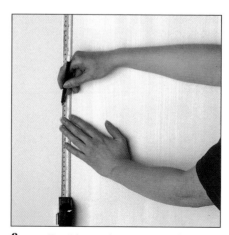

four *Decide on the spacing of the stamps and lightly mark the positions on the wall.*

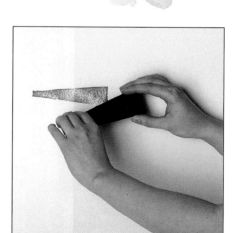

five *Put some black paint on to the plate and evenly coat the small roller. Roll the paint on to the stamp. Stamp the design in the marked positions.*

BEAUTIFUL BEDROOM

WHO WOULDN'T WANT TO SLEEP in this lavender-grey and white bedroom? These two cool colours have a calming effect. The frieze is stamped in white at dado (chair) rail height on a lavender-grey wall. The simple reversal of the wall colours on the headboard provides both contrast and continuity. You can stamp on to an existing headboard or make one quite simply from a sheet of MDF (medium-density fiberboard) cut to fit the width of the bed. Use the stamps to make matching accessories and make the most of them by using only the central part of the tendril stamp on the narrow border of a picture frame.

YOU WILL NEED

drawing pins (thumbtacks)

string

spirit (carpenter's) level

emulsion (latex) paint: white and lavender-grey

foam rollers

tendril, grape and leaf stamps

headboard or sheet of MDF (medium-density fiberboard) painted white

masking tape

pencil

straight edge

broad, square-tipped artist's paintbrush

one *Use a drawing pin (thumbtack) to attach one end of the string in a corner of the room at dado (chair) rail height. Run the string along the wall to the next corner and secure the end. Check the string with a spirit (carpenter's) level and adjust if necessary.*

two *Spread white paint on a plate and run a roller through it until evenly coated. Ink all three stamps and stamp a tendril, grape and leaf in sequence along the wall, aligning the top edge of each stamp with the string. When the first wall is complete, move the string to the next wall and continue all the way around the room.*

three *To decorate the headboard, stick masking tape around the top and side edges of the white board.*

four *Spread lavender-grey paint on to a plate. Stamp alternate leaves and tendrils down both sides of the board.*

◄ five *Ink all three stamps and stamp a tendril, leaf and grape along the top of the board and repeat the sequence to complete the row. Check the spacing before you stamp; wide spacing is better than squashed motifs.*

six *Measure a central panel on the board and lightly draw it in pencil. Stick strips of masking tape around the panel and the border. Mix some lavender-grey and white paint, then paint the border and the central panel in this colour.* **►**

SUN WALLPAPER

HANDPRINTED WALLPAPER is the ultimate luxury and costs a fortune, but you can make your own at a fraction of the cost. This project requires a certain amount of planning and a long, clear work surface, such as a wallpaper-pasting table. Fast-drying emulsion (latex) paint is used, but even so, care must still be taken to avoid smudging the pattern as you move along the paper. Measure the walls to be covered, adding approximately 2m (2yds) to allow for pattern matching. Inexpensive lining paper was used here, but there are finer-quality plain papers on the market that you may prefer.

YOU WILL NEED

straight edge

felt-tipped pen

sun motif rubber stamp

paper strip the width of the wallpaper

pencil

small paint-mixing tray or plate

turquoise green emulsion (latex) paint

small rubber roller

wallpaper paste (made up according to the manufacturer's instructions)

wallpaper pasting brush

one *With the straight edge, draw lines that butt up against the extremities of the sun stamp. Extend these around the sides of the stamp, so the exact position of the shape is marked.*

two *Make a measuring guide by marking out the width of six stamps along the paper strip.*

three *Place the measuring guide along the bottom edge of the wallpaper. Pour a little paint in the mixing tray or on a plate and run through it until evenly coated. Ink the stamp with the paint. Make a test print to check that it is not overloaded.*

four *Make the first stamp print in the second section, the next in the fourth and the last in the sixth, lining them up along the measuring strip.*

five *Place the paper measuring strip along the side of the wallpaper, making light pencil marks as a guide. Reposition the paper strip horizontally and print the next row of motifs in the first, third and fifth sections. Move the stamp up, using the vertical pencil marks as a guide and print the third row in the same positions as the first. Continue in this way until the wallpaper is completed.*

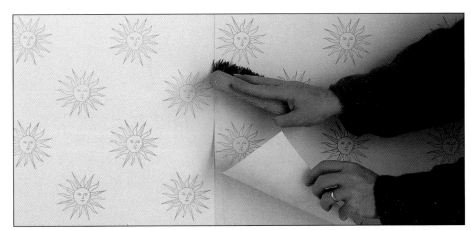

six *Hang the wallpaper to form a continuous pattern, matching up the rows of suns with the final row resting on a dado (chair) rail.*

MEXICAN HALLWAY

BANISH GLOOMY WEATHER with vibrant sunshine-yellow and intense sky-blue in the hallway, and then add an ethnic touch by stamping an Aztec border along the walls. Use the patterns from the template section to cut basic geometric shapes from a medium-density sponge. Mix shades of green with purples, add an earthy red and then stamp on diamonds of fuchsia-pink for sheer brilliance. Try not to be tempted by muted colours for this border, as it will lose much of its impact. Make a bold statement. Bright colours go well with natural materials, such as straw hats, sisal matting, wicker baskets and clay pots.

YOU WILL NEED

tape measure

spirit (carpenter's) level

pencil

emulsion (latex) paint:

sunshine-yellow and deep sky-blue

paint rollers

paint-mixing tray

foam strip

medium-density sponge cut into the pattern shapes from the template section

emulsion (latex) paint:

light blue-grey, purple, brick-red, fuchsia-pink and dark green

5 plates

one *Divide the wall at dado (chair) rail height, using a tape measure, spirit (carpenter's) level and pencil. Paint the upper part sunshine-yellow and the lower part deep-sky blue, using a paint roller. When dry, use the spirit (carpenter's) level and pencil to draw a parallel line about 15cm (6in) above the blue section. Create the foam shapes using the templates at the back of the book as a guide.*

two *Use a foam strip to stamp a light blue-grey line directly above the blue section and another along the parallel marked line.*

three *Spread an even coating of each of the frieze colours on separate plates. Use the rectangular and triangular shapes alternately to print a purple row above the bottom line and below the top line.*

four *Stamp the largest shape in brick red, lining it up to fit between the points of the top and bottom triangles. There should be about 1cm (½in) of background colour showing between the brick red and purple.*

◄ **five** *Stamp the diamond shapes in fuchsia-pink between the central brick-red motifs.*

six *Finally, add a zig-zagged edge by printing dark green triangles along the light blue-grey lines.* ➤

GEOMETRIC WALL-BOARD

YOU DO NOT NEED to be an artist to make a work of art for your wall and even make sure it's the right size and in complementary colours for the room! With a piece of MDF (medium-density fiberboard), a simple, repetitive design and a little patience, you can create a wall decoration at little cost. A stencil is all that's needed and, if you stick to a design made of simple squares and circles, it is no problem to create your own stencil. Alternatively, it is worth looking at the commercial stencils available. There are so many designs to choose from, you are certain to find one you like.

YOU WILL NEED

scrap paper

pencil

ruler

pair of compasses (compass)

MDF (medium-density fiberboard)

safety mask

tape measure

saw

emulsion (latex) paint: blue, yellow and red

paintbrushes

acetate sheet

craft knife

self-healing cutting mat

masking tape

stencil brush

small artist's brush

eraser

clear varnish & brush

screw eyelets

picture-hanging wire & hook

hammer

drill, with masonry and wood bits (optional)

wall plugs (optional)

wood screws (optional)

one *Choose your colours. You may consider complementing your existing furnishings. Plan out the whole design to scale on paper. Here, a wrapping paper design was used for inspiration.*

two *Cut the board to size, apply the blue base coat and allow to dry. Draw a grid of squares on the painted surface. Use a ruler and compasses (a compass) to draw the stencil on the sheet of acetate. Cut out the stencil carefully using the craft knife on a cutting mat.*

three *Tape the stencil over one of the squares on the grid. Stencil all the yellow circles and surrounds, then stencil the red circles and surrounds.*

four *Touch up any smudges with the artist's brush. When the paint is completely dry, rub out (erase) any visible pencil lines.*

five *Apply a coat of varnish. Attach the wall-board to the wall by inserting screw eyelets and stringing picture-hanging wire between them. Hammer in a strong picture hook and hang the board as you would a painting. Alternatively, drill holes in the wall and insert wall plugs, screw the board to the wall and fill and make good the screw holes.*

STENCILLED FLOOR TILES

THIS ATTRACTIVE REPEATING PATTERN is derived from an ancient Greek mosaic floor. Painting a floor in this way on individual tiles before they are laid puts much less strain on the back and the knees than other techniques. Cork tiles absorb colour well. It is best to use only a small amount of paint and build it up in layers if necessary. Make two stencils from the template at the back of the book, one for each colour, so that they do not get mixed. A wide variety of effects can be created by changing the colour combinations or using more than two colours, in which case, additional stencils will be required.

YOU WILL NEED
graph paper
ruler
pencil
pair of compasses (compass)
stencil card (stock)
craft knife
self-healing cutting mat
masking tape
30cm (12in) cork tiles
spray adhesive
stencil paints: terracotta and blue
stencil brushes
acrylic sealer

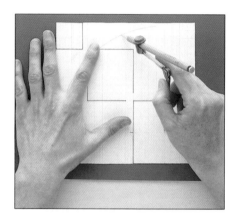

one *Enlarge the quarter section template at the back of the book so that it will fit within a 15cm (6in) square. Using graph paper will make the design more accurate. Rule the three squares and draw the curves with a pair of compasses (compass). Rub all over the pencil lines on the back with a pencil.*

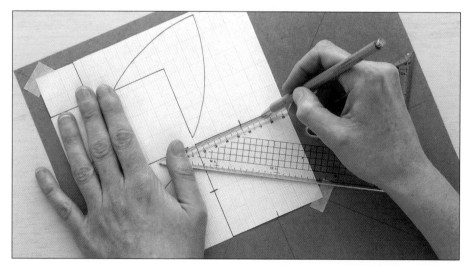

two *Cut two 30cm (12in) squares from stencil card (stock), draw four lines from corner to corner and edge to edge. Divide the card into eight equal segments. For the first stencil, tape the graph paper, face up, to one corner of a piece of card and draw around the corner and centre square to transfer the design. Repeat on each corner, turning 90 degrees each time. Cut out five squares. For the second stencil, draw along the curves and around the remaining square. Cut out eight shapes.*

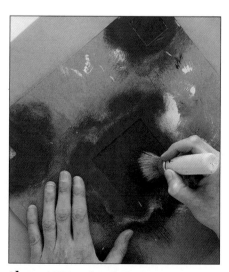

three *Wipe the tile to remove any dust and spray the back of the first stencil with adhesive. Stencil the squares with terracotta paint. Leave to dry.*

◄ **four** *Using the second stencil and blue paint, complete the design. Stencil the remaining tiles in the same way and leave to dry.*

five *When the tiles are complete and dry, spray with acrylic sealer to make them waterproof. Adhere them to the floor following the manufacturer's instructions carefully.* ►

CORK-STAMPED FLOOR

THIS STAMP HAS been made from seven wine bottle corks. They have been taped together in a daisy shaped bundle and the pattern shapes are cut from the surface of the cork bundle with a scalpel. Dense cork like this is a good material to carve into, being both soft and very smooth. Use the stamp on dust-free sanded wood, or on cork tiles with a dark woodstain. Allow it to stand and soak up the stain for ten minutes, then blot it on kitchen paper towels before you begin printing. Use the paper strips to ensure that the pattern is an even distance from the wall.

YOU WILL NEED
7 wine bottle corks
wood glue or PVA (white) glue
strong adhesive tape
felt-tipped pen
scalpel
2 paper strips of equal width
dark woodstain
bowl
kitchen paper (paper towels)

one *Glue the corks in a daisy formation, standing the ends flat on a piece of paper. This will provide a level printing surface. Bind the corks together with strong adhesive tape once the glue has become tacky.*

two *Draw the pattern on to the cork surface with a felt-tipped pen. Cut out the background pieces with a scalpel.*

three *Start by making one stamp at each corner, placing the paper spacing strips against the skirting as guides.*

four *Move the strips along the straight skirting board (baseboard) section and stamp a motif about halfway between the first two. Stamp a row of evenly spaced motifs between the existing prints. Continue to stamp a border all around the room.*

STAMPS AND DRY BRUSH

SOMETIMES, WITH A ROOM that has unusual furnishings, it is worthwhile giving it a further distinctive style by making a design statement on the walls or floor. Here, the busy look of dry brush strokes combines with the elegant simplicity of Japanese calligraphic characters. The result is a warm and uniquely stylish look that makes a memorable room.

YOU WILL NEED

calligraphy brush

ink: black and rust

white paper

scissors

paper glue

foam block

craft knife

hammer

masking tape

emulsion (latex) paint:
cream, rust and white

large and small paint rollers

dry paintbrush

matt (flat) varnish

one *Paint your Japanese characters with the calligraphy brush first, following the examples shown in this project. Make photocopies of each design. Cut the characters out roughly and glue one of each character to the foam. Keeping the knife at an angle, cut away all the white paper and the foam underneath it, to make a raised stamp.*

two *Prepare the floor, hammering in any protruding nails. Ensure that it is clean and dry. Mask off both edges of alternate boards. Apply a base coat of cream paint and allow to dry.*

three *Draw a dry brush, dipped into a little neat rust paint, across the unmasked boards in a series of parallel strokes, allowing the base coat to show through in places. Repeat this exercise with white paint, which softens the whole effect. Leave to dry, then repeat the procedure with both colours on the remaining boards.*

four *Plan your design of Japanese characters, using spare photocopies of the characters, roughly cut out. Using a small roller, ink some of the stamps with black ink. Replace some of the photocopies with black stamped characters.*

five *Repeat, using the rust-coloured ink. Seal well with matt (flat) varnish and allow to dry.*

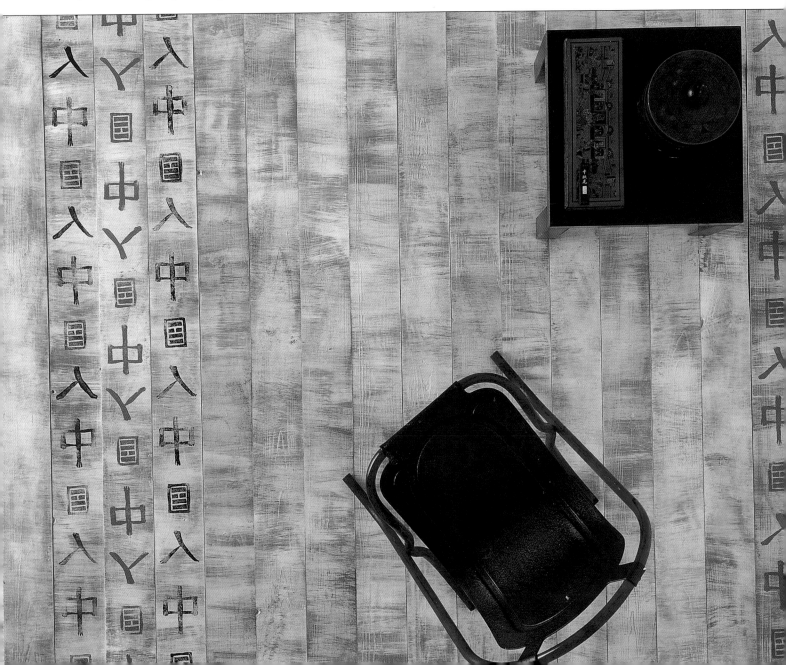

STAMPED HORSE BORDER

ADD EXTRA INTEREST to a painted floor or wall with this simple border pattern. Cutting the stamp isn't difficult, but works best if you use high-density foam, the type used for camping and exercise mats. Don't attempt to cut right through the foam the first time. Apply the paint to the stamp with a paint roller. If you simply press the stamp into the paint, it will absorb too much. Practise on paper before starting the border to build up your skills.

YOU WILL NEED

sanding machine

power sander and sandpaper

horse template

tracing paper

pencil

spray adhesive

square of 1cm (½in) thick high-density foam

craft knife

ruler

wood stain:

light blue and white

medium household paintbrush

dark blue emulsion (latex) paint

small gloss paint roller

paint-mixing tray

clear matt (flat) polyurethane varnish and brush

one *If your floor is unpainted, sand with a hired sanding machine and finish with a hand-held power sander.*

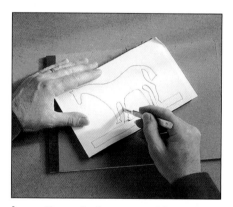

two *Trace the horse motif from the back of the book. Spray the back lightly with adhesive and stick it on top the piece of foam. Using a craft knife, "draw" a cut around the horse.*

three *Make another angled cut to meet the first, then pull away a thin strip of foam from the edge of the horse, revealing the outline. Cut through the full depth of foam. Peel off the paper.*

four *Place the stamp on the floor to help determine the width of the border, a little way out from the wall.*

five *Paint the strip of floor by the wall with blue wood stain. When dry, paint the border with white wood stain. Stain the rest of the floor blue.*

six *Pour some dark blue paint into the paint tray. Run the roller through to coat evenly and apply paint to the stamp. Start stamping at a corner or focal point. Stamp all around the room, changing the angle slightly each time to vary the effect. When dry, seal the floor with two coats of varnish.*

PHOTOCOPY MONTAGE

THIS EFFECT IS REMINISCENT of the painted floors of the great European palaces. Few of us can afford to commission frescoes and floor painting, but we might still aspire to a home decorated in a style fit for Marie Antoinette. Using photocopied images on a freshly prepared floor can turn these dreams into reality. Choose any theme: the photograph shows a composition of landscapes, but architectural drawings, classical motifs, such as columns, urns and statues, or even a still-life of fruit or vegetables could be made into successful montages. Using the same techniques, you could create a totally modern feeling using colour photocopies of, say, flower heads; instead of stencilling the borders, add freehand leaves and scrolls if you are skilled.

YOU WILL NEED

eggshell emulsion (satin-finish latex) paint: cream and green

paintbrushes

photocopied images

long metal ruler

craft knife

self-healing cutting mat

artist's watercolour or acrylic paints

gum arabic tape (optional)

pencil

masking tape

acetate sheet

bleed-proof paper (such as tracing paper)

green stencil paint

stencil brush

wallpaper paste

matt (flat) varnish

one *Starting with a well-prepared hardboard or marine-plywood floor, paint on an undercoat of cream eggshell paint, followed by a top coat. Allow to dry completely.*

two *Experiment with images in different sizes and settle on an arrangement that looks good on your floor. Trim the images so that you are left with just the pictures.*

three *If your images are black and white, use watercolour or acrylic paints to put soft washes of colour over the prints. You may need to stretch the paper, using gum arabic tape, depending on the quality of the paper (test a small area first).*

four *Arrange the images on the floor and plan and draw out the borders. Mask off the boxes for the images with masking tape. Paint between the lines of masking tape with green eggshell paint. When the paint is almost dry, gently peel off the masking tape.*

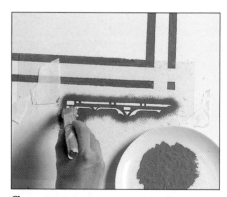

five *Make the stencil from the template at the back of the book with the acetate sheet. Apply the stencil to the floor with masking tape and stipple with green paint. Glue the photocopies to the floor with wallpaper paste. Varnish the floor several times.*

MEDALLION FLOOR

FLOOR STENCILLING, like this American folk art design, began in imitation of expensive, oriental rugs, ·in the same way that stencilled walls imitated fine printed wallpaper. Floorboards were often made of pine, which was then painted with layers of oil paint to prevent them from splintering, and then stencilled with borders and repeat patterns. These patterns were often more intricate and colourful than the patterns on walls and on a larger scale, sometimes 30cm (12in) wide.

YOU WILL NEED

sugar soap or all-purpose cleaner

matt emulsion (flat latex) paint: olive green and black

household paintbrushes

stencil brush

tape measure

tracing paper

pencil

acetate or stencil card (stock)

craft knife

spray adhesive

masking tape

matt (flat) polyurethane varnish

one *Prepare the surface by washing it with sugar soap or cleaner. When dry, apply two coats of green paint, leaving each one to dry.*

two *Trace the template from the back of the book. Transfer to acetate or stencil card (stock) and cut out with a craft knife. Measure the floor to judge how many medallions will fit comfortably between each corner. Lightly spray the back of the stencil with adhesive and begin by stencilling a medallion in each corner and one midway between them.*

three *Stencil one row of medallions all around the room and use as a guide for positioning the others. The grid can be broken up by using the centre of the motif between each block of floor. Use masking tape to isolate the centre and make a small stencil to fill in the gaps. When dry, seal the surface with two or three coats of varnish.*

TEMPLATES

The templates may be resized to any scale required. They can be enlarged or reduced using a photocopier.

Star stencil
page 66

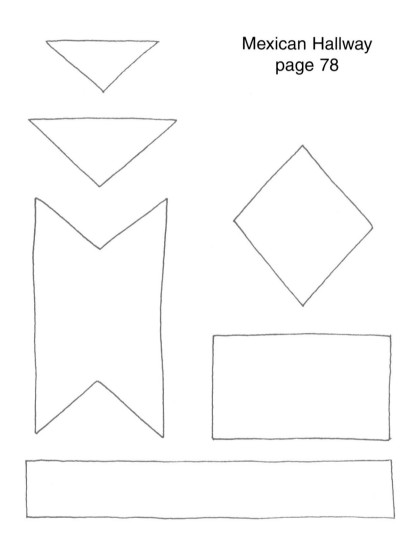

Mexican Hallway
page 78

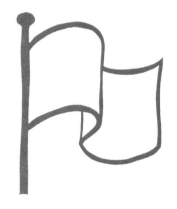

Flag stencils
page 68

Cork-stamped
Floor
page 84

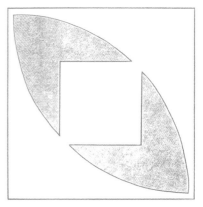

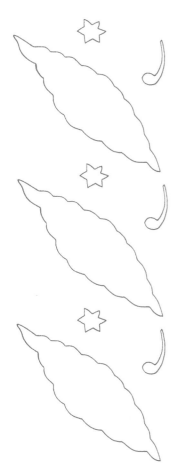

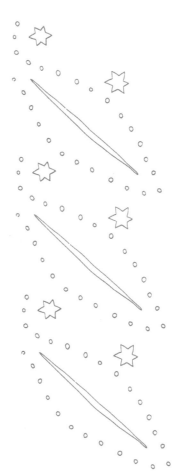

Stencilled Floor Tiles
page 82

Stencilled Border
page 70

Medallion Floor
page 92

Stamped Horse Border
page 88

Photocopy Montage
page 90

INDEX